The Wellington Bomber Story

The Wellington Bomber Story

Martin W. Bowman

The History Press

Published in the United Kingdom in 2011 by
The History Press
The Mill · Brimscombe Port · Stroud · Gloucestershire · GL5 2QG

British Library Cataloguing in Publication Data
A catalogue record for this book is available from the British
Library.

Hardback ISBN 978-0-7524-6193-9

Typesetting and origination by The History Press
Printed in China

CONTENTS

The 'Wimpy', as the Wellington was universally known, operated in every theatre of war, serving as a tactical and strategic bomber by day and by night; as a maritime reconnaissance machine; as an anti-submarine aircraft; as a minelayer; as a torpedo-bomber and as a transport, dropping supplies to partisan groups in occupied Europe. Though it did not have a high ceiling or an exceptional range it could be dived at speeds well beyond its design specification without losing a wing, as more than one crew found in their endeavour to evade a prowling night-fighter. It could haul a 4,000lb 'Cookie' bomb to targets in the heart of Nazi Germany. This was due mainly to the aircraft's light weight and its geodetic construction, which conferred immense strength and was capable of withstanding severe punishment without

➤ *Wellington B.I (K4049), the Wellington prototype which flew for the first time on 23 December 1937. (Vickers)*

➤➤ *Wellington B.I (K4049) on an early test flight. (Vickers)*

its structural integrity being destroyed. This form of lightweight, robust and seemingly complex lattice structure had been used by Mr Barnes Neville Wallis of Vickers in the design of the R 100 airship in 1930. Wallis then joined Vickers' aeroplane division at Weybridge as chief engineer (structures) and used geodetic construction for the first time in a heavier-than-air aircraft including the Wellesley two-seat monoplane bomber. It was this aircraft that demonstrated clearly the excellent weight/strength ratio of such structures when, in November 1938, two specially prepared Wellesleys flew from Ismailia, Egypt to Darwin, Australia, non-stop in just over 48 hours and setting a new world long-distance record of 7,157.7 miles. Wellesleys entered service with Bomber Command in the spring of 1937. The 2,000lb bomb load

▶ Wellington I fuselages in the Weybridge erecting shop. (Vickers)

▶▶ Wellingtons of 149 Squadron over Paris on Bastille Day, 14 July 1939. (IWM)

was carried in streamlined nacelles to avoid breaking up the internal geodetic pattern of the fuselage. The bomb-stowage problem would be overcome in 1936 in Vickers' next geodetic-structure type to appear, a medium bomber conforming to the Air Ministry specification B.9/32.

On 20 October 1932 the Air Ministry had invited Vickers (and Bristol, Gloster and Handley Page) to submit a design study for an experimental twin-engined day bomber powered by Rolls-Royce Goshawk evaporation-cooled engines and capable of carrying a bomb load of 1,000lb for 720 miles, with a range of 1,500 miles. R.K. Pierson and his team decided to use the ingenious geodetic framework devised and developed by Barnes Wallis in the design of the new high-wing monoplane bomber, which would have a fixed undercarriage.

But by October 1933 Pierson proposed using a retractable undercarriage and geodetic construction throughout the aircraft, because the geodetic latticework construction had by now reached such a stage that it could be incorporated in the airframes of large aircraft. Geodetics offered an unobstructed space between the front and rear spars outboard of the engine nacelles and it was agreed later that three separate petrol tanks would be installed in each wing. A revised specification included front, rear and midships gun mountings with wind protection and a mid-wing configuration was chosen to give a better view to pilots flying in formation. The bomb undershields were modified, spring-loaded bomb doors were added and the oil system was also revised.

The Goshawk proved to be one of the few Rolls-Royce failures and another design study using Rolls-Royce Merlin engines was carried out, but in August 1934 use of the more powerful 915hp Bristol Pegasus X engines, which gave a speed of 250mph at 8,000ft, was agreed with the Air Ministry, who wanted to increase the fuel load to provide a range of 1,500 miles at 213mph at 15,000ft. The Pegasus engines were fitted with de Havilland-Hamilton two-pitch type variable-pitch propellers. A Vickers-Supermarine Stranraer-type fin and rudder saved design time. Following wind tunnel tests conducted by Vickers, their own nose and tail 'cupolas' with hand-operated single guns in each were also accepted, both front and rear gun turrets being glazed over with Plexiglas. There was

Did you know?
In September 1940 Wellington production was at the rate of 134 a month and by the spring of 1941 had grown to more than double this figure.

*The front turret of a Wellington gets a final polish of its Perspex by an RAF sergeant. (*Flight*)*

An engine fitter attends to a Pegasus XVIII. (IWM)

The Mk.II prototype which was used to test the Vickers 40mm cannon installation.

Did you know?
The 11,461st and final Wellington, a T.10 built at Squires Gate, Blackpool, was delivered on 13 October 1945. Altogether, 3,406 Wellingtons were built at Blackpool.

provision for a third gun with a retractable shield to be mounted in a dorsal position half-way along the fuselage. A crew of four was provided for, with allowances for one supernumerary for special duties. The permitted bomb load was nine 500lb bombs or nine of 250lb for long-range operations.

The B.9/32 prototype finally flew at Brooklands on 15 June 1936 with Vickers chief test pilot Captain J. 'Mutt' Summers at the controls, accompanied by Barnes Wallis and Trevor Westbrook. A series of trials proved successful and the prototype was exhibited in the New Types Park at the annual RAF display at Hendon on 5 June 1936. The RAF were particularly impressed with its ability to carry double

Did you know?
In 1939 British Airways (the pre-war airline eventually merged with Imperial Airways to form BOAC) discussed a civil version of the Wellington for use on the West African route, with the possibility of an extension across the South Atlantic.

the bomb load and cover twice the range (3,000 miles) that was originally specified. In August 1936 the Air Ministry placed an initial production order for 180 of the Vickers Type 271. Vickers suggested the name 'Crecy' but Wellington would be adopted in September 1937 because while it was correctly named after a town according to Air Ministry nomenclature, Wellington also perpetuated the memory of the 'Iron Duke' and followed tradition in that its geodetic predecessor bore the Duke's family name, Wellesley. On 29 January 1937 Specification 29/36 was issued to cover the first production run of 185 Wellingtons, powered with 1,000hp Pegasus XVIII engines. Allowance was made for the Pegasus XXs in event of delays in developing the two-speed

supercharger intended for the XVIII. The Wellington I was a complete redesign with a deeper fuselage and accommodation for a larger bomb load and an increase in crew to five. The nose was lengthened to accommodate the revised gun turret and bomb aimer's position. The redesigned horizontal tail unit of high-aspect ratio removed the horn balances of the B.9/32. Elongated side windows were incorporated into the fuselage, which was increased in length. Wingspan was also extended slightly. Constant speed propellers and a retractable tail wheel were fitted and Vickers nose and tail turrets and a Nash & Thompson ventral turret were installed.

On 19 April 1937 the prototype crashed during diving trials when excessive load caused the failure of the horn balance and

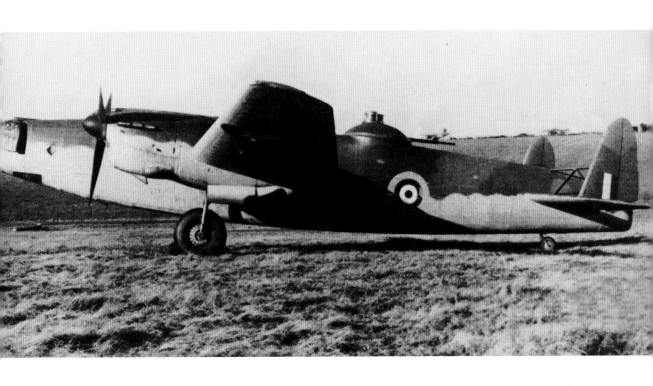

▶ *Wellington I L4212 production prototype in flight. This aircraft first flew on 23 December 1937, powered by Pegasus XX engines. (Vickers)*

▶▶ *Wellington I L4317 served on 115 Squadron and later 15 and 12 OTUs before becoming an instructional airframe in March 1942. (Vickers)*

Wellington I L4280 over the River Wey during its approach to Weybridge in 1938. (RAF Museum)

the aeroplane turned on to its back. The pilot was thrown through the roof of the cockpit and escaped by parachute but the flight engineer was killed in the crash. The fuselage and tail surfaces were revised by the time the first production Type 285 Wellington B.I (K4049) first flew at Brooklands on 23 December 1937. During February and March 1938 an undercarriage failure caused by the misalignment of a toggle strut grounded the aircraft. While repairs were being carried out, the Pegasus XVIII was installed. On 10 October 1938 99 Squadron became the first in Bomber Command to receive the Wellington I. In 1939 production of 189 examples of the B.IA began. Both Vickers turrets were replaced by Nash & Thompson and each was equipped with two .303in machine guns (as was the existing ventral position). Various other improvements were made and the crew complement was increased to six. The IB proposed as a result of difficulties experienced with the armament did not enter production.

The first of 2,685 Type 415 B.IC versions of the Pegasus XVIII began entering squadron service before the outbreak of war. The hydraulic system was redesigned and a 24-volt electrical system to operate the DR (directional radio) compass was introduced. One of the most important modifications introduced on the IC, subsequently incorporated on all Marks, was the substitution of Vickers K machine guns in the midships position in place of the ventral turret, and the addition of larger main wheels which protruded

from the engine nacelle when retracted. IC required tremendous forward pressure on the control column to bring the nose down when going round again with flaps down. A characteristic of the Wellington was to drop its nose during turns.

BY DAY AND BY NIGHT

Did you know?
One of the best-known and most widely used aircraft types of the Second World War, the Wimpy operated from the first RAF raid of the war, on 4 September 1939, right through to March 1945.

Navigator at his station. The crew of early Wimpys consisted of two pilots, observer (who was also responsible for aiming the bombs), wireless operator/air gunner and rear gunner. Another gunner might also be carried to man the front turret.

When war was declared on 3 September 1939, 3 Group of RAF Bomber Command was equipped with six front-line Wellington I and IA squadrons in East Anglia and two reserve squadrons. The following day fourteen Wellingtons attacked the battle cruisers *Scharnhorst* and *Gneisenau* at Brünsbuttel but bad weather and heavy anti-aircraft fire interfered with the action and two of the bombers were shot down. Crews that scored hits on the vessels discovered that the general-purpose bombs, fused for eleven-second delay, simply bounced off the armoured decks and fell into the sea without exploding.

On the night of 8 September three Wellingtons were despatched to drop propaganda leaflets over Hannover. One aircraft was forced to abort but the other two successfully completed the operation.

The Wellington (and Blenheim) crews were rested while Hampden squadrons bore the brunt of bombing raids in East Anglia. Ground crews used the time to iron out the bugs and eliminate teething troubles inherent in the Wellington IA, which had been introduced almost overnight into squadron service. By December heavy losses in British merchant shipping prompted the War Cabinet to order Bomber Command to mount, as soon as possible, 'a major operation with the object of destroying an enemy battle-cruiser or pocket battleship' but 'no bombs are to be aimed at warships in dock or berthed alongside the quays'. The War Cabinet wanted no civilian casualties caused as a direct result of bombing. On 3 December 24 Wellingtons attacked units of the German fleet at Heligoland from 'high' level in cloud. All returned

Wellington I crew prepare for an operation over enemy territory. (IWM)

9 Squadron Wellington Is in formation in 1939. (IWM)

safely but when on 14 December twelve Wellingtons penetrated the Schillig Roads near Wilhelmshaven at low level they came under heavy fire from warships, flak-ships and fighters. The Wellingtons maintained formation but five were shot down and one crashed when almost home, against the loss of one enemy fighter. The Air Staff put on a brave face, saying that, '...The maintenance of tight, unshaken formations in the face of the most powerful enemy action is the test of bomber force fighting

Did you know?

During the Second World War no other British bomber was built in greater numbers – 2,515 Wellingtons were built at Weybridge and the rest at 'shadow' factories at Chester and Blackpool.

efficiency and morale. In our service it is the equivalent of the old "Thin Red Line" or the "Shoulder to Shoulder" of Cromwell's Ironsides…' AVM 'Jackie' Baldwin AOC 3 Group compared the disaster to the Charge of the Light Brigade. The Luftwaffe pilots registered five kills, plus one probable, for the loss of one German fighter shot down.

On 18 December twenty-four Wellingtons were attacked near Heligoland by forty-four German fighters alerted by radar, and the Wimpys were under

27

Wellington P2515 of 37 Squadron which was downed by flak during a Nickel (leaflet) raid near Eifel on 23 March 1940.

➤ *Setting out. (IWM)*

almost continuous attack until 80 miles from home on the return flight. Twelve Wellingtons and eleven complete crews were shot down. Two more were written off in crashes and three others were damaged in crash-landings in England. Twelve German fighters were claimed shot down but just three Bf 109 fighters were lost. On 2 January 1940 when twelve Bf 110s attacked three Wellingtons, two of the bombers were shot down and a third had a lucky escape. Armour plate was now quickly installed and self-sealing fuel tanks were fitted. The Vickers turrets had insufficient traverse and the 'dustbin' ventral turret was useless against beam attacks from above. At long last the RAF admitted that unescorted bombing by day was not feasible, but darkness would prove no greater ally than daylight had been.

The RAF night offensive had opened in February 1940 with 'Nickel' raids, involving propaganda leaflets, or 'Bumphlets', being dropped on Germany. They at least provided an opportunity for crews to gain

➤ *Sergeant James Ward of 75 Squadron RNZAF, who was awarded the Victoria Cross for his actions on the night of 7–8 July 1941, when the target was Münster. (IWM)*

some valuable experience of flying at night. It would not be until March that Bomber Command was allowed to bomb land targets for the first time. Wellington ICs were issued to 149 and 99 Squadrons. Crews, ever-mindful of the beam attacks made by the Luftwaffe, soon installed hand-held machine guns in the long narrow side windows. Wellington ICs were first used on 20 March during a sweep over the North Sea. Next day they made a night reconnaissance over Germany. On 23 March Wellingtons reconnoitred the River Elbe and the port of Hamburg. One crew, which lost its way, was shot down by anti-aircraft fire near Dunkirk. On 7 April Wellington crews were brought to a state of readiness after German ships had been sighted heading for Norway and Denmark as part of an invasion force. An attempt at

bombing by two squadrons of Wellingtons was thwarted by bad visibility. On 12 April twelve Wellingtons searched for German warships off the Norwegian coast near Stavanger but none were sighted and they were intercepted by Me 110s. Again employing beam attacks to excellent advantage, they shot down two of the

▲ Wellington II W5461 of 104 Squadron at Driffield, which failed to return from Berlin on the night of 12–13 August 1941. (IWM)

➤ *Wellington L4387/ LG-L of 215 Squadron on detachment with Coastal Command which, on 12 April 1940 and with extra fuel tanks in the bomb bay, was used by a crew on 75 Squadron RNZAF to carry out a reconnaissance north of Narvik. The Wellington returned safely to Wick 14 hours and 30 minutes after leaving – a record for an operational sortie that was not surpassed for some time. (IWM)*

➤➤ *Wellington crews back from a raid. (IWM)*

33

Wellingtons. Twelve other Wellingtons which attacked two cruisers, the *Köln* and the *Königsberg*, in Bergen harbour, fared little better. None of their bombs did any lasting damage. The next bombing operations were made at night on the airfield at Aalborg in Denmark where the Luftwaffe had established a large supply base for their Norwegian campaign. On 17–18 April 75 Squadron despatched three Wellingtons to Stavanger for its maiden bombing operation. Two aircraft managed to bomb the target. On 25 April, when six Wellingtons attempted another raid on Stavanger, it proved abortive. Thereafter, the Wellingtons were again employed on North Sea sweeps and night reconnaissance operations over the island of Sylt to prevent mine-laying seaplanes from operating.

Finally, on the night of 14–15 May Wellingtons bombed a German target when Aachen was attacked and the following day the War Cabinet authorised attacks east of the Rhine. On the night of 15–16 May Bomber Command began its strategic air offensive against Germany when ninety-nine bombers, thirty-nine of them Wellingtons, bombed oil and steel plants and railway centres in the Ruhr. Throughout May the Wellingtons attacked tactical targets with limited success. Italy's decision, at midnight on 10 June, to declare war on Britain and France caused Bomber Command to send Wellingtons and longer-range Whitleys to bomb heavy industry in the north of Italy. On the night of 16–17 June only five of the nine Wellingtons despatched were able to find and attack

the Caproni works at Milan. After France sued for an armistice all future operations were brought to an end.

During July 1940 Wellingtons carried out attacks on west and north-west Germany, with the occasional raid on targets in Denmark. On the night of 23–24 August the Luftwaffe bombed London; the first raid on the capital since 1918. On 24–25 August eighty-one Wellingtons, Hampdens and Whitleys were detailed to bomb Berlin as a reprisal. The flight involved a round trip of 8 hours and 1,200 miles. Seven aircraft aborted and twenty-nine bombers claimed to have bombed Berlin. A further twenty-seven overflew the capital but were unable to pinpoint their targets because of thick cloud. Five aircraft were lost to enemy action, including three which ditched in the North Sea. Berlin was again bombed on the night of 30–31 August. In September Wellingtons made repeated night attacks on invasion barges massed in the Channel ports ready for Operation Sealion, the proposed German invasion of England.

Design of the Wellington II with Rolls-Royce Merlin X in-line engines had begun in January 1938, but a delay in production of the engine meant that the prototype (L4250) did not fly until 3 March 1939. As a result of experience gained operating the I and IA, a larger tail-plane and a stronger undercarriage with larger-diameter wheels were introduced. Performance proved superior to that of the IC and enabled a higher all-up weight, so that a greater load of bombs or increased range by carrying more fuel could be attained and higher ceiling and cruising speed allowed modification to carry a 4,000lb 'block-

buster' bomb. A total of 400 Wellington IIs were built and these were followed by 1,519 Mk.III models. The prototype (L4251), with air-cooled 1,400hp Bristol Hercules III engines, flew for the first time on 16 May 1939. Other features which became standard were de-icing gear, balloon cutters and windshield wipers. The mock-up of a four-gun FN-20A turret was installed in the tail while the FN5 nose turret

△ Wellington T2470/ BU-K of 214 Squadron at Stradishall being towed in for repairs in October 1940. (IWM)

Wellington II Sri Guroh, one of several Wellingtons paid for by funds raised in the Malay States, of 214 (Federated Malay States) Squadron at Stradishall, Suffolk, in November 1941. (IWM)

and beam guns remained unchanged. The new and more powerful four-gun FN-20 tail turret was first carried in about March 1940 by L4251. The Wellington II and III both entered production in 1940.

Entering service on 9 Squadron on 22 June 1941, the Wellington III was destined to be the backbone of Bomber Command until such time as the four-engined Stirlings, Halifaxes and Lancasters appeared in sufficient numbers to take over.

A decision had been taken early in 1937 that New Zealand would have a complement of thirty Wellingtons, six of

The rear gunner and pilot of a 149 Squadron Wellington, safely back at Mildenhall, examine the damage caused to their aircraft by a German night-fighter, possibly during the raid on Kiel, 19–20 August 1941. During the attack, the fabric covering the rear fuselage caught fire, and the rear gunner had to use his parachute pack to beat out the flames. The unique geodetic construction enabled Wimpys to take such punishment in their stride.

R1006 H-Harry of 301 (Polish) Squadron about to be bombed up at Swinderby in November 1940. (IWM)

which would be ready to leave for the Antipodes in August 1939. When war clouds gathered 75 Squadron RNZAF was put at the disposal of the RAF. On 5 August 1941 Sergeant James Ward RNZAF, the second pilot of a 75 Squadron RNZAF Wellington, was awarded the Victoria Cross for his actions on the night of 7–8 July

◄◄ *Wellington crews of 75 Squadron RNZAF at Feltwell in early 1941. (British Official)*

◄ *A Czech bomber crew in February/March 1941. (IWM)*

R1593/OJ-N of 149 Squadron in April 1941 at Mildenhall being loaded up with 250lb HE bombs.

'Weary Willie' of 149 Squadron at Mildenhall in May 1941. (British Official)

when the target was Münster. On the return flight at 13,000ft over Ijsselmeer the Wellington, which was piloted by Squadron Leader Reuben Widdowson, was attacked by a Bf 110 night-fighter. The rear gunner was wounded in the foot but managed

➤ *Corporal Basil Wilson, engine fitter Grade 1, about to take a test flight on Wellington IC P-Pointer of 109 Squadron at Boscombe Down in 1941. (Paul Wilson)*

to drive off the enemy aircraft. Incendiary shells from the fighter started a fire near the starboard engine and, fed by a fractured fuel pipe, soon threatened to engulf the whole wing. The crew tied a rope around Ward's waist and he climbed out of the astrodome into a 100mph slipstream in pitch darkness a mile above the North Sea. By kicking holes in the fabric covering of the geodetics he inched his way to the starboard engine and smothered the fire, which threatened the whole aircraft. Ward was KIA on 15–16 September 1941 over Hamburg.

During 1941 and 1942 109 Squadron (formerly the Wireless Intelligence Development Unit) was designated the Wireless Intelligence Special Duty Squadron. It had a number of different types of aircraft, all fitted with special radio-intercept equipment. Wellingtons had been introduced in January 1941 and were used especially on the longer-distance flights, both by day and by night. The Wellington was invaluable in the radio-intercept role, finding and pinpointing German radio beams used in their blind bombing systems. On 8 May 109 was able to prove the existence of nine sites along the French coast of an advanced type of Fighter Control radar, capable of much greater accuracy than earlier models. This resulted in one, the site at Bruneval, being raided and dismantled by Combined Operations forces in 1942. 109 were also used in the interception of the German battleship *Bismarck* on 27 May 1941.

Did you know?

The Wellington II was used for several years to test tail-mounted Whittle jet engines and the later Mk.VI wings were installed allowing the aircraft to attain a height of 36,000ft.

Germany's occupation of Norway, the subsequent overrunning of France and the Low Countries and Italy's intervention in the war changed the situation in the war at sea radically. The only salvation available to RAF crews was ASV (Air to Surface Vessel) radar. Relatively few aircraft in Coastal Command were fitted with the device and those that were did not always perform as efficiently as crews would like. Ideally, a U-boat had to be fully surfaced and no more than 3 miles distant for ASV to be effective. Early in 1941 221 Squadron, at Bircham Newton, Norfolk, equipped with Wellington Is, began receiving ASV sets and in March the squadron began receiving

➤ *Leigh Light Mk.XIV Wellington with underwing rockets. (IWM)*

Wellington IC of 311 (Czech) Squadron and Whitleys at dispersal at Talbenny on the coast of St Bride's Bay in 1943. (Bill Cameron)

GR.VIIIs. A total of 271 Wellington IC aircraft were modified to GR.VIII day torpedo bomber and night anti-submarine bomber configuration, equipped with ASV II search radar to meet the threat posed by enemy surface ships and U-boats, largely

in the Mediterranean. By May 1941 the U-boats were largely reduced to operating off West Africa or in the central Atlantic, the latter being beyond the range of Coastal Command aircraft. By September increased shipping losses resulted in large numbers of Wellington bombers and other types being used in the war at sea. 221 Squadron moved to Iceland, returning in December for transfer overseas. Three crews flew their GR.VIIIs to Malta while the remainder of the squadron flew to Egypt in January 1942 to begin anti-shipping patrols from bases in the Canal Zone.

In the spring of 1942 the first Wellington GR.VIIIs powered by Bristol Pegasus XVIII

◄ *Wellington GR.XIV of the TRE (Telecommunications Research Establishment). (IWM)*

▶ *A GR.XIV and crew of 304 (Polish) Squadron. (IWM)*

Did you know?

DWI (Directional Wireless Installation) Wellingtons carried generators with which to create an electromagnetic field generated from an aluminium coil encased inside a cumbersome circular 51ft-diameter balsa wood structure outside the aircraft. These were used to destroy enemy mines at sea.

▲ *Wellington GR.XIV MP818. (RAF Hendon)*

engines entered service with Coastal Command. Just over two years earlier, ICs had taken part in maritime operations for the first time when Wellington DWIs, fitted with 48ft-diameter dural hoops, had been employed in exploding enemy magnetic mines at sea. Altogether, 394 GR.VIII 'Stickleback' Wellingtons, nicknamed 'Goofingtons', were built, fifty-eight of which carried Leigh Lights. Very early in the war Coastal Command had realised that its anti-submarine aircraft would need

▲ *Blackpool-built Wellington XIII 'Stickleback' torpedo-bomber. (RAF Museum)*

something more reliable than the quickly consumed flares they were using at night to illuminate U-boats. In 1940 Squadron Leader H. de B. Leigh experimented with a 24in airborne searchlight in the dustbin turret of a DWI (Directional

Wireless Installation) Wellington, complete with generator. Leigh had his prototype installation ready by January 1941. By May the first successful trials were carried out and any weight problems were overcome by substituting batteries for the generator. The Leigh Light operator had to switch on the light at the last possible moment just as the ASV reading was disappearing from the radar screen because the blip, which grew clearer up to about three quarters of a mile from the target, then became merged in the general returns from the surface of the sea. The detached object was then trapped and held in the beam allowing the crew to release its bombs. The use of radio altimeters provided very accurate indication of the 50ft height at which the light should be turned on in order to pick out a U-boat. The Leigh Light eventually won acceptance over the heavier Helmore Turbinlight which proved totally unsuitable for anti-submarine work.

During April 1942 Coastal Command received a squadron of Whitleys, eight Liberators and a Wellington squadron (311 Czech), and 1417 Flight at Chivenor was expanded to become 172 Squadron, but by May only five Leigh Light Wellingtons had arrived. On 7 May 304 (Polish) Squadron arrived at Tiree in the Inner Hebrides. 304 commenced operations on 18 May and 311 Squadron three days later, from Aldergrove in Northern Ireland. The Poles moved on 13 June to Dale in South Wales to join 19 Group Coastal Command. They flew 2,451 sorties up until 30 May 1945 and attacked thirty-four U-boats out of forty-three sighted. 311 operated the Wellington until June 1943 when it converted to the Liberator.

➤ 311 (Czech) Squadron crew beside their Coastal Command Wellington. (IWM)

➤➤ 221 Squadron Wellington XII with ASV radar operating from Malta in January 1944. (Shaw)

Wellington XIII 'Stickleback' torpedo-bombers. (RAF Museum)

On the night of 3–4 June 1942 a Wellington of 172 Squadron illuminated the Italian submarine *Luigi Torelli* in the Bay of Biscay and badly damaged it with depth charges. The same Wellington also strafed another submarine with machine-gun fire, having used all its depth charges on the first attack. During the remainder of June the

Wellington XIIIs at CNS Shawbury in August 1944. (RAF Museum)

five Leigh Light Wellingtons sighted seven U-boats in the Bay of Biscay. Whitleys, using conventional methods, failed to find any enemy vessels during the same period. The Leigh Wellingtons proved so successful that on 24 June Admiral Dönitz ordered all U-boats to proceed submerged at all times except when it was necessary to recharge batteries. Although the number of confirmed successes was destined to be relatively small, the morale of U-boat crews slumped with the knowledge that darkness no longer afforded them protection. On the night of 5–6 July Leigh Light Wellingtons recorded their first U-boat kill when Pilot Officer W. Howell, an American, sank *U-502* in the act of battery-discharge while crossing the Bay of Biscay.

The GR.XI torpedo bomber was equipped with ASV II, which had only a 1.5m wavelength and a row of four large external aerials mounted along the fuselage spine and two rows of four 'T' aerials mounted along each rear fuselage side. In every other respect, externally the GR.XI was essentially similar to the Mk.X. By January 1943 Coastal Command aircraft had almost ceased to locate U-boats by night and so ASV II was replaced with the long overdue ASV III, an American version of 10cm wavelength, developed with the help of British scientists. Provision was made for the GR.XI to carry ASV III, which required a re-design of the aircraft's nose. ASV III had been successfully tested in May 1942 but British models would not be available until spring 1943. In total, 180 GR.XI airframes were built at the Weybridge (105) and Blackpool (Squires Gate) (75) factories. These were followed on the production lines at Chester and Weybridge by fifty-eight GR.XII anti-submarine examples. These were equipped with ASV III which was not dependent on external aerials, the radar gear being housed in a chin radome beneath the nose. The FN-5 nose turret was deleted and replaced by a clear nose canopy containing a pair of flexible Browning machine guns. Both the XI and XII versions were powered by Hercules VI or XVI power-plants. Beneath the wing provision was made for two 18in torpedoes

and a retractable Leigh Light was installed in the bomb bay.

844 GR.XIII daylight torpedo bombers were equipped with externally mounted ASV II and powered by two 1,735hp Bristol Hercules XVII engines, the highest-rated engines to power the Wellington; all but two of them were built at Squires Gate. These aircraft operated in Europe and the Mediterranean. After the war eight were sold to Greece. The final general reconnaissance version was the GR.XIV, a total of 841 being built at Chester (538), Weybridge (53) and Squires Gate (230). These were similar to the GR.XIII and were also powered by Hercules XVII engines.

On 15 November 1943 415 Swordfish Squadron RCAF moved to Bircham Newton, Norfolk, for operations using Leigh Lights to illuminate targets for its Albacores to attack E-boats. In 1944 U-boats fitted with Schnorkel equipment enabled them to recharge their batteries at periscope height and sightings were few. Large numbers of XIVs flew operations during spring 1944 and by June Coastal Command operations had reached a peak, with the priority task of keeping the English Channel free of German shipping in preparation for the Normandy invasion on 6 June. At least one U-boat was sunk by a Wellington XIV of 304 Squadron. At the end of the war GR.XIVs were sold to France and were used in the same role as Coastal Command.

Some Coastal Command Wellingtons served as 'flying classrooms' after conversion to T.XVII and T.XVIII standard. The T.XVII was based on the conversion of an Mk.XI under the designation Wellington T. XVII, intended for training night-fighter crews. It carried a Mosquito-type bulbous nose covering an SCR720 Airborne Intercept radar set, replacing the FN-5 nose turret. The rear turret was removed and faired over. The T.XVIII was externally similar to the T.XVII and was internally fitted with radar and wireless equipment with which to train radio operators and navigators. Eighty aircraft were completed under this designation at Blackpool. The T.XIX was a service conversion of the Mk.X, which fulfilled the duties of a basic Wellington bomber crew trainer. While the T.XVI and the T.XVIIs used Hercules XVII engines, the T.XIX bomber trainers were powered by both Hercules XVI and XVII engines. Reversion to the continuous fuselage window strip was a feature of the T.X, as was the retention of the rear turret, although minus guns.

On 22 February 1942 Air Marshal Sir Arthur Harris was appointed C-in-C RAF Bomber Command. A new British directive calling for 'area bombing' of German cities had been received seven days before; the Air Ministry having decided that bombing the most densely built-up areas would produce such dislocation and breakdown in civilian morale that the German home front would collapse.

➤ *H for Harry on 12 Squadron at RAF Binbrook on the night of 25–26 February 1942, when this aircraft failed to return from an operation to Kiel.*

Harris planned to send 1,000 bombers to a German city and wipe it out with incendiaries and when 'Operation Plan Cologne' went ahead on 30–31 May 1942,

599 of the aircraft were Wellingtons (over 300 of them drawn from Operational Training Units and Training Command). In all, 898 crews claimed to have hit

Wellington crews of 103 Squadron at Elsham Wolds, Lincolnshire, on 30 January 1942. (IWM)

➤ *Warrant Officer T.E. Mellor's crew of 196 Squadron at Leconfield on 28–29 June 1943 when they had completed a total of 234 trips between them. 196 operated in 4 Group, Bomber Command for only ten months in 1943, and for five of these months Wellington Xs were flown. (IWM)*

◄ *Wellington IIIs at 30 OTU Hixon, Staffordshire, on 11 September 1943. (IWM)*

Did you know?
While the Dam Busters raid on 16–17 May 1943 was carried out by Lancasters, the initial tests of delivering the cylindrical mine used to destroy the dams were conducted in December 1942 by a Wellington III (BJ895) which was specially modified to carry two of the scaled-down Upkeep weapons.

Cologne and fifty-three bombers were lost. At nightfall on 1 June 956 aircraft – 545 of them Wellingtons (including 347 aircraft from the OTUs) – took off for Essen. Of the thirty-seven bombers lost, twenty were claimed by night-fighters. On 25–26 June

A Wellington IC of 301 (Pomeranian) Squadron. (IWM)

the third and final 'thousand' raid took place when 1,067 aircraft (472 of them Wellingtons) set out for Bremen. Forty-eight aircraft were lost.

In 1942 eleven Wellington squadrons re-equipped with four-engined bombers and one was transferred to Coastal Command. By March 1943 seven Canadian

◀ *Wellington XVII NC869 with Hercules engines. (RAF Hendon)*

Wellington squadrons were operating in 4 and 6 Groups of Bomber Command. During 1943 twelve Wellington squadrons converted to other bomber types and two were transferred to the Middle East. On the night of 8–9 October the last Main Force bombing operation by Wellingtons was made by 300 (Polish) Squadron, during a

▲ A tail gunner with his personal insignia
for any Luftwaffe night-fighter closing in
from the rear. (IWM)

➤ Aircrew of 460 Squadron RAAF on 21 April 1942. In fifty bombing, nine mine-laying
and two leaflet-dropping raids, 460 Squadron lost twenty-nine Wellingtons – the highest
percentage loss of all Bomber Command Wellington units. (Cal Younger)

A Polish crew in front of Wellington II Z8343 of 305 Squadron. Note the bomb log painted above the fin flash. (RAF Museum)

115 Squadron was one 3 Group unit that did not convert to Stirlings, retaining its Wellingtons until March 1943 and flying more Wellington sorties than any other squadron in Bomber Command. It also suffered the highest losses with the type – more than 100, including crash-landings. After thirty-six raids X3662/KO-P was retired to serve on 20 OTU. It was lost in a ditching off Skye on 8 October 1943.

Wellington X LP264 of Telecommunications Flying Unit at Deptford in late 1943. (Zdenek Hurt)

◀ *Wellington III X3763 of 425 'Alouette' Squadron RCAF which failed to return from a raid on Stuttgart on 14–15 April 1943. (IWM)*

▲ *Wellington R1230 NZ-E of 304 (Polish) Squadron, one of seven Wimpys which failed to return from a raid on Essen on 11 April 1942. (RAF Museum)*

In June 1943 Leconfield in Yorkshire was home to two 4 Group squadrons: 196 and 466 RAAF, both equipped with the Wellington X. Y-Youngers receives some attention to its engines. The aircraft's name was chosen by its pilot, Pilot Officer R. Young, and navigator, Sergeant R. Young! Foaming tankards replace the more usual bomb symbols to indicate fourteen successfully completed operations. (IWM)

◄ *An Australian crew of 466 Squadron RAAF who completed their tour on 30–31 August 1943, the penultimate operation before the squadron was stood down to convert from Wellingtons to Halifaxes. Wellington HE984 Snifter has its insignia of Hitler, Mussolini, Goering and Goebbels confronted by a canine puddle. Nose armament had been discarded at this stage in the war and the turret sealed. (IWM)*

➤ *Wellingtons of 300 (Masovian) Squadron at Hemswell, 17 June 1943. (IWM)*

▼ *Wellington B.III PH-B W5358 of 12 Squadron, which crashed at Binbrook on 25 July 1941, was repaired and served later on 158 Squadron at Driffield as T-Tommy, being lost on the night of 12–13 April 1942 when it crashed near Cologne on the operation to Essen. (IWM)*

Ground and flight crews of Wellington X HE472 B-Bambi of 192 Squadron in 100 Group at RAF Foulsham, Norfolk. (Group Captain Jack Short)

◄ *Wellington VR-Q Z1572 in flight. (Charles E. Brown)*

82

raid on Hannover. However, Wellingtons continued to serve on the OTUs of 7 Group throughout 1944-45 and 192 Squadron joined 100 (Special Duties, later Bomber Support) Group to investigate German radio and radar signals from the Bay of Biscay to the Baltic and along all bomber routes using three Mosquitoes, two Halifaxes and eleven Wellington Xs. On the 2,000th night of the war on 3–4 March 1945 when the Main Force bombed the synthetic oil plant at Kamen and the Dortmund-Ems

Canal, sixty-one aircraft of 100 Group took part in counter-measures or 'spoofing' operations and from various OCUs thirty-five Wellingtons and other aircraft flew a Sweepstake diversionary flight towards the Frisian Islands.

Wellingtons also served until the end of the war with the 2nd Tactical Air Force in England and France. In 2nd Tactical Air Force 69 Squadron was unique in that it used Wellingtons for photo-reconnaissance at night. In all, Wellingtons flew 47,409 sorties in Bomber Command, losing 1,386 aircraft on operations and 341 in operational crashes. Only the Halifax and Lancaster squadrons lost more.

◀ *Vickers Wellington of a Polish Squadron. (IWM)*

It was, perhaps, in the Middle East that the Wellington achieved its greatest fame, remaining a front-line bomber almost until the end of the war. When Italy had declared war on Britain and France on 10 June 1940 the RAF was poorly equipped for the defence of Egypt and the Suez Canal and only a few Directional Wireless Installation (DWI) Wellingtons were in place for minesweeping duties. An IA (P2516) was converted at the end of 1939 to carry a large electrically energised hoop of 48ft in diameter as an enemy magnetic mine destroyer and the type was successfully used for this duty in British coastal waters and later in Mediterranean harbours and the Suez Canal.

On 19–20 September 1940 Wellingtons of 70 Squadron made their first attack on the port of Benghazi and the so-called 'mail run' to that vital supply port for General Rommel's Afrika Korps continued almost nightly for several months. For the remainder of 1940, throughout 1941 and for most of 1942, during the ebb and flow of the desert battles, the Wellingtons of 205 Group attacked targets of various types. In November 37 and 38 Squadrons' Wellingtons were despatched to Egypt via Malta to help replace squadrons sent to Greece. The two squadrons helped push back the Italians in the Western Desert and were ably assisted by 148 Squadron, which was despatched from Luqa on Malta on occasion to bomb targets in Tripolitania.

Two Wellington Squadrons – 142 and 150 – operated in 330 Wing of the British North African Air Force and they played an important part in the night-bomber operations during the Tunisian Campaign,

◄ *Wellington X9889 of 40 Squadron at Gibraltar in late 1941. (IWM)*

➤ *Lining up the two-torpedo load for a ship-hunter Wellington in the Middle East. (IWM)*

▲ *Wellington XIIIs in Egypt in 1942. (IWM)*

January until May 1943. The universal thought was that operations in Africa would be 'a piece of cake' compared to flying night-bombing raids over the Ruhr. Two squadrons of Wellingtons would only make a small impact on the land battle but any bombers were welcome at this time. By the end of June 1943 330 Wing was reinforced by four squadrons of Wellingtons from the

DWI Wellington of 1 GRU in Egypt in 1944. (IWM)

Middle East and the arrival at Kairouan/ Zina in Tunisia of 420 'Snowy Owl', 428 'Ghost' and 425 'Alouette' RCAF Squadrons from England. The night-bomber force now assumed quite formidable proportions and 100 Wellington raids began operating

extensively in support of the assaults on Sicily and Italy. During this phase they made a number of remarkably successful attacks on railway bridges in Italy, using 4,000lb delayed-action bombs dropped from very low level. At the end of October all three Canadian squadrons returned to the UK to convert to the Halifax. The establishment of airfields in southern Italy that same month enabled the remaining Wellington squadrons of 205 Group to move to airfields in the Cerignola area.

During the Anzio landings in February 1944 205 Group harassed enemy troop movements behind the German lines, sometimes twice nightly. In April the Wellingtons attacked concentrations of German troops in the Yugoslav town of Niksic and 'Gardening' operations – intensive mining of the River Danube – began. At first sorties were flown only when there was a full moon as the aircraft had to fly no higher than 200ft and even as low as 40–50ft. On the night of 8 April nineteen Wellingtons of 178 Squadron and three Liberators dropped forty mines near Belgrade. Over the next nine days 137 more mines were dropped and in May

On 22 February 1943 Major General James H. Doolittle, commanding the North West African Strategic Air Force, flew in A-Apple on a raid on the docks at Bizerte. (IWM)

Wellington X HE227 at Blida. (RAF Museum)

The Hercules engine on this 424 'Tiger' Squadron RCAF Wellington X comes in for some attention from Canadian ground crew in Tunisia late in 1943. (Harold Hamnett)

An Arab boy and his donkey with Wellington XIII HZ879 Johnny 2 at Relizane, Algeria in November 1943. (Alan Smith)

The Backbone of the RCAF, Bully Beef of 424 'Tiger' Squadron RCAF at Kairouan-Zina in July 1943. (Harold Hamnett)

Wellington 'W' Madame X and P/O Walker RNZAF's crew of 150 Squadron on 20 August 1944. (Les Hallam)

▼ Merlin-engined Wellington IIs on 148 Squadron at Kabrit. (RAF Museum)

➤ Wellington II of 104 Squadron under attack on Malta. (RAF Museum)

Wellington VIII, a victim of unwelcome attention by the Luftwaffe during a bombing raid on Malta. (RAF Museum)

Wellington LN858 of 150 Squadron in 205 Group, which was shot down by Oberleutnant Hans Krause of 6./NJG 101 during a raid on Budapest on 3–4 April 1944 and crashed in Lake Balaton. (Nigel McTeer)

the total number dropped had risen to over 500. By May coal traffic had virtually ceased and canals and ports were choked with barges. On the night of 1 July fifty-three Wellingtons and sixteen Liberators dropped 192 mines in the biggest operation of the mining campaign. The following night another sixty mines were dropped. By August 1944 the volume of material transported along the Danube had been reduced by 70 per cent.

In January 1945 70 and 104 Squadrons began re-equipping with Liberator VIs. On 21 February 205 Group flew the last of its operations using purely Wellingtons and on the night of 13–14 March 1945 Wimpys flew their last operation, when six Wellingtons accompanied a force of Liberators in an attack on the marshalling yards at Treviso, northern Italy.

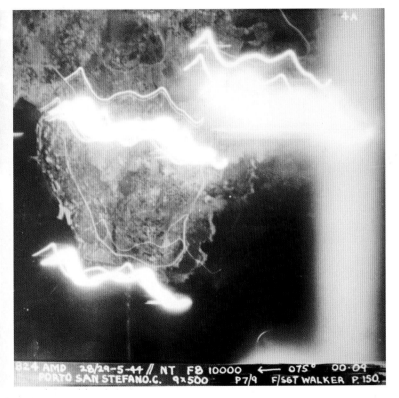

Porto San Stefano taken from 10,000ft on the night of 28–29 May 1944 from Flight Sergeant Walker's Wellington of 150 Squadron. (Roy Gristwood)

Flash photo of Fiume torpedo factory taken from 7,300ft on the night of 21–22 January 1944 from Flying Officer Lyn Clarke's Wellington of 142 Squadron. (Roy Gristwood)

3,803 Wellington X aircraft – more than 30 per cent of all Wellingtons produced – were built at Blackpool (1,369) and Chester (2,434) using recently introduced light alloy parts which matched the strength but not the weight of standard mild steel components. Although all-up weight reached 36,000lb, the general performance was about the same as the Mk.III except that bomb load was reduced from 4,500 to 4,000lb. The Mk.X was powered by Hercules VIs or XVIs with lengthened carburettor intakes on the cowlings and bell-shaped spinner fairings that were absent on the Mk.III. Squadron deliveries commenced late in 1942 and by March 1943 twelve squadrons were either partially or fully equipped, but its use as a first line bomber in Europe was comparatively brief; in 1943 all were replaced by four-engined bombers and the type was deployed to the Mediterranean and the Middle and Far East. In Italy 205 Group only relinquished the Wellington X after September 1944 and in the Far East 99 and 215 Squadron's Wellington Xs were replaced

by Liberators during August and September 1944. Not only did the Wellingtons attack Japanese airfields and supply dumps, but during the critical Imphal battle of mid-1944 both squadrons were used to ferry bombs to Hurri-bomber squadrons operating from the Imphal Plain against the main Japanese supply lines. Wellingtons also flew anti-submarine operations in the Far East until the end of the war.

A Wellington IC (R1220) powered by 1,050hp Pratt & Whitney R1830-S3C4-G Twin-Wasps became the Mk.IV prototype, making its maiden flight in December 1940. Hamilton Standard propellers were used initially but their excessive noise saw them replaced with Curtiss electric propellers. An unfortunate crash-landing of the prototype during its landing approach was later traced to carburettor failure. The Mk.IV was essentially similar to the IC with FN-5 and FN-10 two-gun turrets, although the FN-5 turret was replaced on some aircraft by the FN-20 four-gun turret. A total of 220 production models were built at Chester. Squadron deliveries began in August 1941. Several Wellington IVs were sent to Boscombe Down for general testing and one was equipped with Lindholme Air Sea Rescue gear. A small number of specially equipped photographic reconnaissance Wellington IVs were operated by 544 (PR) Squadron on night photographic experiments over Britain until replaced by Mosquitoes early in 1943.

Late in 1939 Vickers had produced two high-altitude prototypes capable of attaining an altitude of 40,000ft. Both had a special cigar-shaped fuselage with a pressurised cabin in the nose to simulate conditions at 10,000ft. Originally, it was planned to install two 1,650hp Bristol Hercules VIII engines, but production difficulties dictated the use of the 1,425hp Hercules III. The first of the two prototypes (IC R3298) made its maiden flight in September 1940 and achieved a height of 30,000ft but the Hercules engines did not perform as anticipated and development of

the Mk.V was terminated after only three were constructed.

The Merlin 60-powered Wellington VI followed and twenty-eight airframes intended for Mk.V production were built to VIA configuration. The prototype (R3298) flew in September 1940. While the original order placed with Vickers was for 132 high-altitude Wellington Vs and VIs, actual production would be limited to sixty-

▲ *Early Wellington IV R1515 with de Havilland-Hamilton propellers. This aircraft crashed on take-off at Mullaghmore on 20 December 1943.*

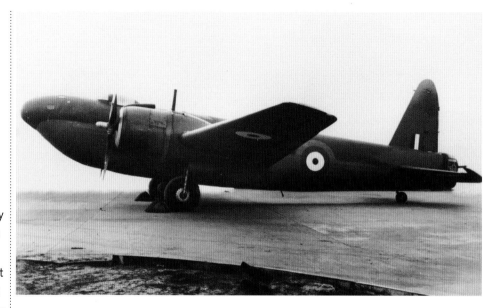

Did you know?
Wellingtons fitted with the embryo airborne part of the *Oboe* system ('Broody Hen') carried out the initial trials of what later became the most accurate British blind bombing system of the Second World War.

seven machines, including the three Mk.V prototypes. Problems of ice accumulation, solidifying lubrication, heating and air-conditioning failures plagued most test flights of the VI, just as they had the V. High-altitude bombing tests were conducted with the Sperry bombsight, with the proposed FN-70 turret being the sole defensive measure. On 19 August 1941 a further 100 VIs were ordered, although fifty-six were later cancelled. The majority became VIs equipped with Gee navigational systems; thirty-two of these VIGs were used either as trainers for, or operators of, the *Oboe* blind target marking device. Late in March 1942 109 Squadron at Tempsford received four Wellington VIs for trials with the *Oboe* radar blind bombing device. By the winter of 1942/43 the need for a high-altitude Wellington ended with the Mosquito, without the need for pressurised cabins, taking on the high-altitude role.

◄ *Wellington VI W5795 dived into the ground from high altitude near Derby on 12 July 1942. (RAF Museum)*

Wellington XIIIs at Sywell, Northamptonshire, in 1945. (RAF Museum)

At one time the Wellington X equipped twenty-five OTUs. With the end of hostilities Wellingtons soon all-but-completely disappeared from the RAF inventory. Several Wellington Xs were revamped by Boulton Paul for extended service as crew trainers with Flying Training Command. This version was known as the T.10 and LP806, belonging to No.1 Air Navigation School, which was finally SOC in March 1953, was the last Wellington in RAF service. A number of T.10s were used to test the high-altitude performance of the Hercules 38 engine fitted with single GEC turbo-blowers. LN718 was powered by Hercules 100 engines, which were intended for use on the Halifax and the Vickers Viking airliner. Noise tests were conducted by Bristol using RP484 whose propellers could be 'feathered'. LN715 had its turrets faired over and was a test-bed for the Rolls-Royce Dart turbo-prop, which would power the Vickers Viscount airliner.

Both the T.10 and the T.19 were superseded in the Air Navigation Schools and at 201 Advanced Flying School at Swinderby by the Vickers Valletta T.3 and the Vickers Varsity respectively. Both the latter aircraft owed their lineage to the wartime Wellington. A redesign of the Viking led to the Valletta for the RAF – a machine first flown in June 1947 which was really 'five aeroplanes in one', because it was capable of quick conversion to a troop carrier, freighter, ambulance, glider tug or paratroop transport. The Valletta was followed by the Varsity 'flying classroom', a specialised crew trainer which took the place of the Wellington T.10, but on an expanded scale.

◀ *Wellington B.X NC844 and HE826 of 2 AGS Dalcross after a landing accident on 20 May 1945. (RAF Museum)*

▶ *Wellington PR.XIII of 69 Squadron over Europe in July 1945. (RAF Museum)*

▲ *Wellington XVI N2875 in August 1944. This aircraft served on 115 and 305 Squadrons and various OTUs before ending its career with CGS on 8 January 1946. (RAF Museum)*

➤ *Vickers Warwick of 38 Squadron, which began equipping with the type in Malta in 1945. The Warwick was designed in parallel with the Wellington. (Henry Fawcett)*

▲ *T.XVIII RP413 wireless and navigation trainer with nose-mounted SCR720 AI radar.*

➤ *C.XVI (IC) transport variant.*

Did you know?

Wellington N2980 *R-Robert* was recovered from Loch Ness on 21 September 1985 after the Loch Ness Wellington Association was formed in 1984. *R-Robert* was lost on New Year's Eve 1940 when it lost its starboard engine minutes after take-off in rapidly deteriorating weather. Squadron Leader Marwood-Elton, the pilot, of 20 OTU at RAF Lossiemouth, ordered his crew to bail out. He spotted a long expanse of water through a break in the thick cloud and decided to ditch. It was Loch Ness. The only casualty was the rear gunner, who died when his parachute malfunctioned.

◀ *Vickers 636 Viking G-AJJN Vulcan, later* Sir Charles Napier, *first flew on 6 April 1947. The Viking used the engine nacelles, undercarriage and, initially, the geodetic outer wings of the Wellington. (via Derek N. James)*

▲ *Wellington T.10 MF628 in flight. (RAF Museum)*

Did you know?

Wellington C.XVs and XVIs were transport aircraft, most of which were converted from ICs by removing the nose and tail turret and installing a fuselage door on the starboard side of the aircraft, midway between the main wing and tailplane. Their bomb bays were sealed and none carried armament.

VARIANTS

Type 271	initial prototype flown on 15 June 1936
Type 285 Wellington I	pre-production prototype with Pegasus X engines flown 23 December 1937
Type 290 Wellington I	183 built with 1,000hp Pegasus XVIII engines. Vickers turrets and 'dustbin'
Type 298 Wellington I	prototype with 1,145hp Merlin X engines, first flown 3 March 1939
Type 299 Wellington III	two prototypes, one with Hercules HE1.sM and one with Hercules III engines
Type 406 Wellington B.II	400 built with Merlin X engines
Type 407 Wellington V	high-altitude prototype with Hercules VIII engines
Type 408 Wellington IA	187 built with Pegasus XVIII engines, Nash & Thompson turrets and 'dustbin'
Type 410 Wellington IV	prototype with Pratt & Whitney Twin Wasp radials
Type 416 Wellington IC	2,685 built
Type 416 Wellington (II)	experimental installation of 40mm Vickers gun in dorsal position applied to original Wellington II prototype

Type 417 Wellington B.III	1,517 built with 1,500hp Hercules XI engines
Type 418 Wellington DWI.I	conversion of one aircraft for mine detonation; Ford auxiliary power unit
Type 419 Wellington DWI.II	conversion of one aircraft for mine detonation; Gipsy Six auxiliary power unit
Type 421 Wellington V	high-altitude prototype with Hercules III engines
Type 423	conversion of all bombers to carry 4,000lb bomb; beam guns and no 'dustbin'
Type 424 Wellington B.IV	220 built with Twin Wasps
Type 429 Wellington GR.VIII	397 built with Pegasus XVIII engines; fifty-eight with Leigh Light; provision for AS weapons, some with provision for torpedoes
Type 432 Wellington VI	prototype with various Rolls-Royce Merlins
Type 435 Wellington IC	conversion of one aircraft to evaluate Turbinlite
Type 439 Wellington II	experimental installation in Wellington II of Vickers 40mm gun in nose
Type 442 Wellington B.VI	sixty-three built with Sperry bomb sight
Type 443 Wellington V	one aircraft converted to Hercules VIII test-bed
Type 449 Wellington VIG	two production aircraft

Did you know?
A Wellington II was used as the test-bed for the Vickers 40mm gun in a dorsal turret which was not put into production. Another Wellington was used to test the Vickers 'S' gun of a similar calibre in a nose-mounted location.

Type 437 Wellington IX	single transport prototype, conversion of IA with Hercules XVI engines
Type 440 Wellington B.X	3,803 built with Hercules VI or XVI engines
Type 619 Wellington B.X	post-war conversion to Wellington T.10; some sold to France and six to Royal Hellenic Air Force in 1946
Type 445 Wellington (II)	test-bed for Whittle W2B/23 turbojet in tail
Type 470 Wellington II	with Whittle W2B
Type 486 Wellington II	with Whittle W2/700
Type 454 Wellington IX	prototype with ASV.II radar and Hercules VI/XVI engines
Type 459 Wellington IX	with ASV III radar
Type 458 Wellington GR.XI	180 built with ASV III and Hercules VI/XVI engines
Type 455 Wellington GR.XII	fifty-eight built with Leigh Light, ASV III and Hercules VI/XVI engines; some sold to France in 1946
Type 466 Wellington GR.XIII	844 built with Hercules XVI engines
Type 467 Wellington GR.XIV	841 built. Hercules XVI engines; many supplied to France during 1944–45 and some sold to France in 1946

Type 478 Wellington X	one aircraft with trial installation of Hercules 100
Type 487 Wellington T.XVII	service conversions to trainers using Vickers kits; Mosquito-type AI radar and Hercules XVII engines
Type 490 Wellington T.XVIII	production version (eighty built) plus some conversions of Wellington XIs; Hercules XVI engines
Type 602 Wellington X	one aircraft as test-bed with Rolls-Royce Dart turboprops

OTHER CONVERSIONS

| Wellington C.XV/XVI | service conversions of Wellington IAs as transports for eighteen troops |
| Wellington T.XIX | service conversions of Wellington X to trainer |

EXPERIMENTAL

| Wellington III | one aircraft with glider-towing clearance for Hadrian, Hotspur and Horsa |

Did you know?
The Mk.III could tow gliders of all types up to the huge Airspeed Horsa and a number of Mk.IIIs were utilised in the early stages of training the British Army's Parachute Brigades. The ventral turret fairing was removed, providing a suitable exit for the trainee parachutists.

SPECIFICATIONS

VICKERS WELLINGTON IC

Crew	Five or six
Powerplant	Two 1,050hp Bristol Pegasus XVIIIs
Performance	Maximum speed 235mph; service ceiling 18,000ft; range 2,550 miles
Weights	Empty 18,556lb; loaded 28,500lb
Dimensions	Wingspan 86ft 2in; length 64ft 7in; height 17ft 5in
Armament	Two nose-mounted .303 machine guns; two tail-mounted .303 machine guns; two .303 beam-mounted machine guns. Bomb load: 4,500lb

VICKERS WELLINGTON B.III

Crew	Six
Powerplant	Two 1,500hp Bristol Hercules XI radial piston engines
Performance	Maximum speed 255mph at 12,500ft. Service ceiling 19,000ft.

Range 1,540 miles with 4,500lb of bombs

Weights   Empty 18,556lb. Maximum take-off 29,500lb

Dimensions   Wingspan 86ft 2in; length 60ft 10in; height 17ft 5in; wing area 840 sq. ft

Armament   Eight .303 machine guns, (two in nose and four in tail turret and one on each beam) plus a maximum bomb load of 4,500lb or one 4,000lb bomb

VICKERS WELLINGTON X

Crew   Five or six

Powerplants   Two 1,675hp Bristol Hercules VIs or two 1,675hp Hercules XVIs

Performance   Service ceiling 22,000ft. Range 2,085 miles

Maximum weight   28,500lb

Dimensions   Wingspan 86ft 2in; length 64ft 7in; height 17ft 5in

Armament   Two nose-mounted .303 machine guns; four tail-mounted .303 machine guns; two .303 beam-mounted machine guns. Bomb load: 4,000lb

ALSO IN THIS SERIES:

Visit our website and discover thousands of other History Press books.

www.thehistorypress.co.uk